P9-DVT-218

Anatomy of a VOLCANIC ERUPTION

by Amie Jane Leavitt

Content Consultant: Steve McNutt, PhD,
Research Professor, Volcano Seismology
University of Alaska, Fairbanks

CAPSTONE PRESS
a capstone imprint

Velocity is published by Capstone Press,
151 Good Counsel Drive, P.O. Box 669, Mankato, Minnesota 56002.
www.capstonepub.com

Books published by Capstone Press are manufactured with paper
containing at least 10 percent post-consumer waste.

Leavitt, Amie Jane.
 Anatomy of a volcanic eruption / by Amie Jane Leavitt.
   p. cm.—(Velocity: disasters)
 Includes bibliographic references and index.
 ISBN 978-1-4296-6022-8 (library binding)
 ISBN 978-1-4296-7357-0 (paperback)
 1. Volcanic eruptions—Juvenile literature. 2. Volcanoes—Juvenile literature. I. Title.
II. Series.
 QE521.3.L43 2012
 551.21—dc22   2011004954

Summary: Describes volcanic eruptions, including their causes, prediction, and effects.

Editorial Credits: Pam Rosenberg
Art Director: Suzan Kadribasic
Designers: Deepika Verma, Manish Kumar, Jasmeen Kaur

Photo Credits
Alamy: Photo Resource Hawaii, cover (back), Ancient Art & Architecture Collection Ltd,
20 (front), Gabbro, 31 (top), The Print Collector, 36, www.BibleLandPictures.com, 37
(bottom), Eric Chahi, 39, imagebroker, 44-45; AP Images: Michael Probst, 34, North Wind
Picture Archives, 40; Dreamstime: Hiroshi Ichikawa, 16 (back); Getty Images Inc: Dana
Stephenson, 23, Richard Roscoe/Visuals Unlimited, Inc, 35; Istockphoto: Henryk Sadura,
31 (middle right), Svengine, 32 (bottom right); NASA: Jacques Descloitres, MODIS Land
Rapid Response Team at NASA GSFC, 12-13, COBE Science Team, 30; Photo Researchers,
Inc: Gary Hincks, 8; Shutterstock: BelarusBSUIR, 7, Skyearth, 9 (bottom), Andrea Danti,
14-15, Billy York, 16 (bottom), Pichugin Dmitry, 18, Steve Bower, 19 (bottom), Vulkanette,
21 (bottom), Zelenskaya, 32 (top right), Juri, 32 (left), Laurence Gough, 33 (top), Pavel
Svoboda, 33 (bottom), PILart, 37 (top), 38, 41, 43 (top); USGS: Austin Post, cover (front),
Lyn Topinka, 17 (bottom), 27 (back), 42-43, G. Iwatsubo, 17 (top), W. Chadwick, 19 (top),
B. Chouet, 20-21 (background), J.P. Eaton, 21 (top), USGS, 22, 31 (bottom), R.P. Hoblitt,
26 (back), D.W. Peterson, 27 (bottom), D. Dzurisin, 28, Terry Leighley, 29, J.D. Griggs, 31
(middle left); Wikipedia: David Karna, 4-5, Gringer, 9 (top), Ed Austin/Herb Jones, 24-25,
Janke, 26 (bottom).

Printed in the United States of America in Melrose Park, Illinois.
032011   006112LKF11

TABLE OF CONTENTS

ERUPTION OF ICY EYJAFJALLAJÖKULL

Small earthquakes shook Iceland's southern coast for four months. Then on March 21, 2010, **lava** began to flow from Eyjafjallajökull volcano. By April 14, another vent opened in the volcano.

Magma inside Eyjafjallajökull pushed its way through the dense rock and thick ice cap. Lava began to pour out. Gas and steam shot tens of thousands of feet high into the atmosphere. Lava spewed from the volcano's **crater** and melted the mountain's glacier. Water rushed down the mountainside. It flooded farmland and wiped out bridges and roads. Darkness covered the area for most of the day.

lava—magma that has reached the surface of Earth
magma—partially melted rock beneath Earth's surface
crater—an indent in the top of a volcano from which lava flows

Airports all over Europe closed after the **eruption** of Eyjafjallajökull. Thick **ash clouds** make it difficult for pilots to see. Ash also damages jet engines. Approximately 100,000 flights were cancelled. Ten million passengers were left stranded until air travel resumed on April 20. It was the largest and longest airspace shutdown since World War II (1939–1945).

eruption—the release of magma, rock, and ash from a vent in Earth's crust
ash cloud—a cloud of hot dust particles and rocks that is formed when a volcano erupts

5

Chapter 1

A VOLATILE PLANET

Earth and Its Many Layers

The Earth we can see is a rocky planet covered by vast oceans and plants. That, however, is just the visible part of Earth. The planet is made of layers which vary in thickness and makeup.

CRUST: The top layer of Earth is called the crust. Earth's crust is made of solid rock. The crust is Earth's thinnest layer. It varies in thickness depending upon location. On the continents, the crust ranges between 19 and 37 miles (31 and 60 kilometers) in thickness. The crust underneath the ocean can be as thin as 3 to 6 miles (5 to 10 km). Earth's crust is made of large pieces called plates. These plates fit together like a giant jigsaw puzzle.

MANTLE: The mantle is the layer directly beneath the crust. This layer is about 1,800 miles (2,900 km) thick. The mantle makes up about 84 percent of the volume of Earth's interior.

The upper part of the mantle is made of partially melted rock called magma. The rocks and magma in the mantle move in circular patterns when they are heated and cooled. These movements are called **convection currents**.

convection current—circular motion in a liquid caused by heating and cooling

CORE: The core is divided into an outer core and an inner core. The outer core is liquid. The inner core is solid. The tremendous amount of pressure in the inner core squeezes the atoms together to form a dense, solid material. The core is about 2,175 miles (3,500 km) thick.

OUTER CORE

INNER CORE

FACT: Scientists can't cut into Earth to find out what it looks like on the inside. One way they can learn about Earth's interior is by studying seismic waves. These are waves that occur during earthquakes.

Where Plates Meet

The plates that make up Earth's crust float on top of the mantle like ships at sea. The plates move because the mantle's rocks are constantly in motion. They don't move quickly, but they move enough to cause changes in Earth's surface over time. Some plates move toward each other. These are called convergent plates.

Convergent Plates

When two plates collide, the denser one moves underneath the lighter one. That's what happens when an oceanic plate collides with a continental plate. The oceanic plate goes underneath the continental plate. Earthquakes are common at these plate boundaries because of the stress created by the collision. The solid rock of the oceanic plate partially melts into magma as it moves deeper into the mantle. This magma is pushed up into the continental plate and forms a volcano. Many volcanoes are found along convergent plate boundaries.

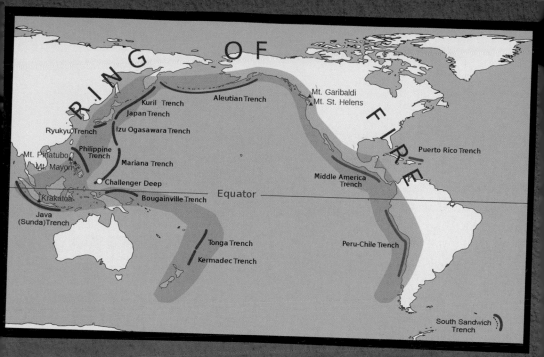

Ring of Fire

One of the most famous convergent plate boundaries on Earth is found in the Pacific Ocean. It is where the Pacific Ocean plate meets with all of the continental plates surrounding it. This area is called the Ring of Fire because more than 450 volcanoes are found there. In fact, 75 percent of all the world's volcanoes on land are found in the Ring of Fire.

Mount Fuji in Japan is part of the Ring of Fire.

Where Plates Pull Apart

Some adjacent plates do not move toward each other. Instead, they pull away from each other. These are called divergent plates.

Divergent Plates

When two plates pull apart, they leave a space between them. This space is quickly filled with magma. It creates a new area of land called a ridge.

DIVERGENT
PLATES

If the magma pushes its way completely out of the ridge, undersea volcanoes are formed. These volcanoes keep growing taller and taller until their tops are out of the water. These new land formations become islands and island chains.

Divergent Plate Boundaries

One divergent plate boundary is found under the Atlantic Ocean. This is where the North American plate and Eurasian plate are pulling apart. Scientists believe that long ago North America and Europe were connected. But after pulling apart for millions of years, they are now separated by a vast ocean. The plates are still moving apart today. The area where the sea floor is spreading is called the Mid-Atlantic Ridge.

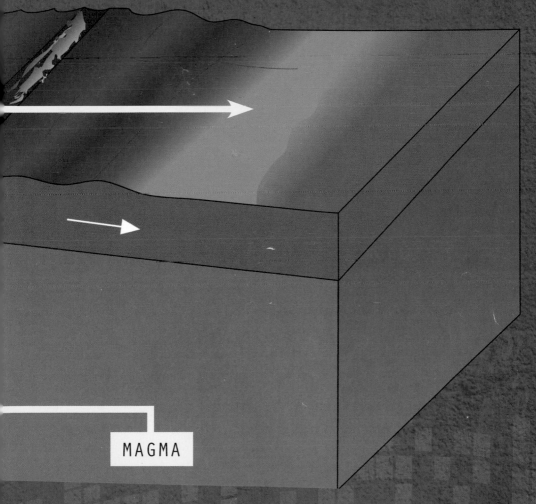

MAGMA

Many volcanoes are found along the Mid-Atlantic Ridge. The island of Iceland contains at least eight volcanoes. Eyjafjallajökull is the volcano that caused all the disruption in air travel in 2010. It is found on the Mid-Atlantic Ridge in Iceland.

Hot Spots

Volcanoes occur where two plates meet. Sometimes they also form in the middle of plates in areas called hot spots. A hot spot is a place where magma rises up through the crust and forms a volcano. If a hot spot is in the ocean, the volcano will eventually grow tall enough to become an island. Over time, a different part of crust will move over a hot spot because Earth's plates are constantly moving. Then a new volcano forms.

The most famous example of a hot spot is the Hawaiian Island chain. Kauai was the first island to form over the hot spot. As the crust moved to the northwest, each additional island was formed. Currently, Hawaii Island is over the hot spot. It is one of the two Hawaiian islands with active volcanoes. Eventually Hawaii Island will move off the hot spot. Another volcano is rising far beneath the surface of the ocean. It is called Loihi and it is located about 19 miles (31 km) southeast of Hawaii Island's Kilauea volcano.

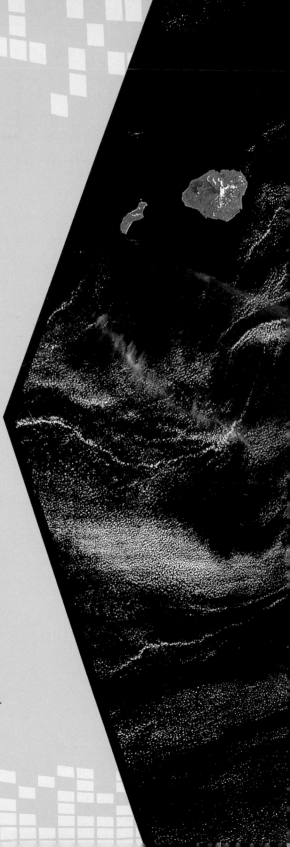

Hot spots don't just occur on oceanic plates. They can also occur on continental plates. Scientists believe a hot spot is what causes the volcanic activity in Yellowstone National Park.

The Hawaiian Islands are volcanic islands that formed over a hot spot.

Chapter 2

FOUNTAINS OF FIRE

VENT: the top opening of the conduit

FLANK: side of a volcano

LAVA

CRATER: an indent in the top of a volcano where the lava flows originate

VOLCANO CLASSIFICATION

ACTIVE VOLCANOES:
Volcanoes that have had at least
one eruption in recorded history.

DORMANT VOLCANOES:
Volcanoes that have not erupted in
historic time, but are expected to
erupt again in the future.

EXTINCT VOLCANOES:
Volcanoes that have not had any
eruptions in the last 10,000 years
and are not expected to erupt again.

ASH CLOUD

SUMMIT: highest
part of a volcano

CONDUIT: a pipe
that magma travels up
to reach Earth's surface

MAGMA CHAMBER: the bottom part
of the volcano where the magma is stored

15

Types of Volcanoes

There are different kinds of volcanoes. These include stratovolcanoes, cinder cones, and shield volcanoes.

STRATOVOLCANOES often take millions of years to form. Numerous eruptions and layers of ash and lava have built up on their sides. They are sometimes called composite volcanoes. Examples include Mount St. Helens, Mount Fuji, Mount Rainier and Mount Hood.

Mount Fuji in Japan

CINDER CONES are the simplest and smallest volcanoes. They are relatively short, usually 1,000 feet (305 meters), or less in height. Many have a bowl-shaped crater at their summit. Most originate from single eruptions.

a cinder cone on the Hawaiian island of Maui

LAVA DOMES form when the lava that pushes out of a conduit is too thick and sticky to move a great distance. It builds up into a round, domed mass of lava. An example of this is the Novarupta Dome in Alaska. Mount St. Helens built several lava domes in its crater after it violently erupted in May 1980.

Novarupta Dome in Alaska

SHIELD VOLCANOES are built up almost entirely of lava flows. They are called shield volcanoes because their shape resembles a warrior's shield. These volcanoes are generally very large and wide. Mauna Loa and Kilauea in Hawaii are examples of shield volcanoes.

Belknap, a shield volcano in Oregon

Other Volcanic Structures

There are other types of volcanic structures besides mountains. These include plugs, mud volcanoes, geysers, fumaroles, and hot springs.

GEYSERS are hot springs that periodically erupt, shooting steam and water into the air. The water is heated by the hot rocks deep in Earth's crust.

Pohutu Geyser, New Zealand

FACT
Geysers can be found on every continent except Antarctica.

FUMAROLES are openings in Earth's crust near a volcano. They are spots where hot steam and other gases escape. Yellow sulfur deposits often encrust the outside of a fumarole. Fumaroles are common on active volcanoes. Increased fumarolic activity on a dormant volcano is a clue that a dramatic eruption may occur in the future.

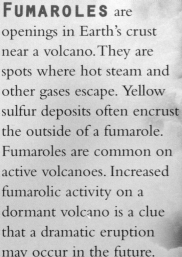

Scientists collect gas samples at a fumarole.

PLUG VOLCANOES are landforms that occur when magma hardens inside the vents of active volcanoes. The magma plugs the vents. Over time the outside part of the volcano is worn away through erosion. Eventually, the plug is all that is left. An example of this landform is Devil's Tower in Wyoming.

Local Native Americans consider Devil's Tower to be a sacred place.

Volcanic Eruptions

Three characteristics are used to categorize volcanic eruptions. They are the amount of material that is released during the eruption, the height of the eruption column, and how long the eruption lasts. There are four major types of volcanic eruptions: Vulcanian, Hawaiian, Strombolian, and Plinian.

VULCANIAN eruptions are named after a volcanic island in Italy called Vulcano. These eruptions spew rock fragments, ash, and hot magma. Their eruption columns can reach as high as 12.5 miles (20 km) into the sky. They are dramatic explosions with material being propelled at speeds up to 1,150 feet (351 m) per second! These eruptions often occur when a lava dome explodes or when magma forcefully pushes a plug out of a volcano's conduit. These eruptions are usually a series of brief pulses that can go on for days, months, and even years.

a statue of the Roman god Vulcan

The word *Vulcan* is Latin and was the name of the Roman god of fire.

HAWAIIAN eruptions are the smallest and calmest of all the volcanic eruptions. They have an eruption column of about 1.2 miles (2 km) or less. They have quick-moving lava flows and don't usually send out much ash. The most unique characteristic of a Hawaiian eruption is the lava fountain. Lava fountains spray liquid lava high into the air.

STROMBOLIAN eruptions are small eruptions that occur at somewhat regular intervals over a period of time. They are named after a volcano in the Mediterranean on the island of Stromboli. This volcano has been erupting about every 20 minutes for hundreds of years. Strombolian eruptions have an eruption column of about 6 miles (10 km) or less in height. They are much noisier than Hawaiian eruptions and only occasionally produce lava flows.

PLINIAN eruptions are named after a Roman soldier named Pliny the Elder. His nephew, Pliny the Younger, wrote an eyewitness account of the aftermath of the eruption of Mount Vesuvius in AD 79. Ever since then, eruptions similar to that of Vesuvius have been called Plinian eruptions.

Plinian eruptions are the largest and most violent type of volcanic eruptions. Their great columns of hot gas and ash can rise as high as 30 miles (48 km) into the air. The largest of these eruptions are called Ultra-Plinian. These deadly explosions look like giant mushroom clouds. Plinian eruptions often result in deadly **pyroclastic flows** and pumice bombs. Often the entire volcanic mountain is destroyed by these massive eruptions.

The eruption of Mount St. Helens in 1980 was a Plinian eruption.

pyroclastic flow—a fast-moving flow of extremely hot gas and rocks from a volcanic eruption

Under the Sea

A **SURTSEYAN** eruption is a volcanic eruption that occurs underwater or very close to the surface of the water. They are similar to Strombolian eruptions but are much more explosive.

An undersea volcano erupts off the coast of Tonga in the South Pacific Ocean.

Volcanic Explosivity Index

Scientists have come up with a chart that helps them compare volcanic eruptions. They look at characteristics such as severity of an eruption and the amount of material in an eruption cloud. They also look at the height of an eruption cloud, the duration of an eruption, and other characteristics. Scientists then give an eruption a Volcanic Explosivity Index (VEI) number. This is similar to the number on the Richter scale that scientists use to describe the size of an earthquake. Check out some famous volcanic eruptions and their VEI numbers.

Yellowstone National Park

Volcanic Eruption	VEI
Kilauea, United States (1962 to 1982)	0
Nyiragongo, Democratic Republic of the Congo (1982)	1
Eyjafjallajökull, Iceland (2010)	2
Galeras, Colombia (1924)	3
Mount Pelee, Martinique (island region of France) (1902)	4
Mount St. Helens, United States (1980)	5
Vesuvius, Italy (AD 79)	6
Tambora, Indonesia (1812)	7
Yellowstone Caldera, United States (2 million years ago)	8

Scientists believe that one of the largest ever volcanic eruptions occurred millions of years ago in what is now Yellowstone National Park. This eruption had a VEI of 8.

The Materials of a Volcanic Eruption

TEPHRA are rock fragments that erupt from a volcano. They vary in size. Larger pieces are called blocks or bombs. They can weigh as much as 30 tons (27 metric tons)! Smaller pieces are called ash.

tephra rock layers

The **ASH CLOUD** of a volcano is made up of volcanic gases and tephra. When this material mixes with water molecules in the atmosphere, acid rain can form.

Mount Redoubt eruption

A **LAHAR** is a volcanic mudflow. It is formed when volcanic material mixes with ice or water in lakes and rivers near the volcano. Lahars are heavy like wet concrete. They can also be very large. A lahar in Washington State near Mount Rainier was 460 feet (140 m) deep.

lahar from the Mount St. Helens 1980 eruption

A **PYROCLASTIC FLOW** is like a snow avalanche except it's made of scorching hot tephra and toxic gasses. This is by far the most dangerous and deadly part of a volcanic eruption. A pyroclastic flow can travel more than 60 miles (97 km) per hour and cover everything in its path with a thick layer of sizzling debris.

lava flow on Kilauea Volcano in Hawaii

LAVA FLOWS come in many different varieties. Scientists group them according to the type of magma the flow is made of. Scientists also consider how hot the lava is and how fast it travels.

Chapter 3

VOLCANOLOGY

Studying Volcanoes

The study of volcanoes and their eruptions is called volcanology. Most volcanologists have graduate and doctorate degrees in geology or volcanology. They work in offices and laboratories. They also work on and near volcanoes.

Geological Investigations

One way volcanologists study volcanoes is by studying a volcano's lava. They measure the temperature of fresh lava. They study the makeup of lava. They also study the age of old volcanic rocks to determine how long ago eruptions occurred.

A scientist studies a lava flow in Hawaii.

Geologists study Mount St Helens.

Seismology Investigations

Many times earthquakes occur before, during, and after volcanic eruptions. Volcanologists study these earthquakes to learn more about volcanic eruptions. Volcanologists use **seismographs** to study earthquakes. These tools give information about the location, size, and strength of an earthquake.

seismograph—an instrument that detects ground motion and measures how strong it is

29

Satellites

Satellites orbit Earth and take pictures of our planet. These pictures give scientists information about events such as volcanic eruptions.

Volcanologists can look at satellite images to track ash clouds, see pyroclastic flows, and determine the size of eruptions. Tracking ash clouds is very important, especially for airlines. Ash clouds are dangerous to fly through. Planes are diverted if scientists determine there's an ash cloud in their paths.

Satellite images also help volcanologists find possible hot spots in Earth's crust. This helps them predict where future volcanic eruptions might occur.

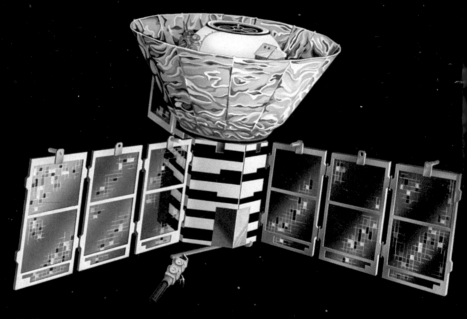

Plate Tectonics

Earth's crustal plate movements account for most volcanic activity on this planet. So volcanologists also study plate tectonics. They examine Earth at convergent plate boundaries and divergent plate boundaries. Volcanoes often produce large local ground movements. Scientists also look at how Earth is moving at fault lines.

VOLCANOLOGY TOOLS

- Seismographs
- GPS instruments
- Video and still cameras
- Infrasound microphones
- Lightning detection equipment
- Infrared cameras
- Cameras on robots
- Thermometers
- Tools that measure volcanic gases

SEISMOGRAPHS

Geologists use a laser device to study a volcano in Hawaii.

GPS UNIT

Water tiltmeters are used to detect changes in the slope of a volcano's surface.

31

Chapter 4

VOLCANIC EFFECTS

The Good

Though they are sometimes violent and destructive, volcanoes provide many benefits for our planet.

MINERALS

Many of Earth's most valuable resources are found in volcanic rock. These include minerals such as fluorine, sulfur, zinc, copper, lead, tin, uranium, tungsten, silver, mercury, and gold.

copper

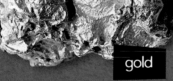

gold

zinc

FERTILE SOIL

The richest soil is often found in places with volcanic activity. That's because volcanic rock is filled with minerals and nutrients that plants need to grow. In Indonesia, for example, farmers can harvest three crops of rice a year in volcanic soil. Farmers planting in non-volcanic soil harvest much less.

NEW LAND

Volcanoes also create new land on Earth. Hawaii Island, for example, is constantly growing.

GEOTHERMAL POWER

Geo means "earth" and thermal means "heat." Geothermal heat is produced in Earth's core and mantle. It heats the rocks and water deep in Earth's crust. People can drill into Earth and use the heated water and steam to produce electricity in power plants.

a geothermal power station in Iceland

FACT Reykjavik is the capital of Iceland. This city of more than 100,000 people is heated almost entirely by geothermal energy.

The Bad

Volcanoes provide many benefits, but they can also cause some problems.

UNUSUAL WEATHER

In 1815, Mount Tambora erupted in Indonesia. It was the world's biggest volcanic eruption in more than 1,600 years.

The next summer, Thomas Jefferson recorded details about the odd weather that the United States was experiencing. The weather was very cold. Snow fell in some parts of New England in June. The entire Northern Hemisphere experienced what is called the "year without a summer." Without warm weather, farmers were unable to harvest a crop that year. Many people suffered as a result.

Scientists believe that volcanic ash from the Tambora eruption caused the year without a summer. The ash blocked out sunlight which in turn cooled down Earth and changed weather patterns.

DISRUPTED AIR TRAVEL

Volcanoes disrupt air travel. This can cause big problems for the global economy. Ash clouds are dangerous for airplanes. Even the smallest particles can cause engine failure if the amount of ash is big enough.

the Frankfurt, Germany, airport during the eruption of Eyjafjallajökull in 2010

The Ugly

The ugly effects from Plinian and Ultra-Plinian eruptions don't occur very often. These huge eruptions cause serious damage.

PYROCLASTIC FLOWS

Pyroclastic flows are the most deadly and dangerous parts of volcanic eruptions. These avalanches of death scorch everything in their paths. They cover the ground in a thick blanket of gray ash and rocks. Nothing is safe in the path of a pyroclastic flow. Plants, animals, and humans can be killed.

This forest in Chile was damaged by a pyroclastic flow in 2008.

LAHARS

Volcanic mudflows are common in eruptions. These heavy walls of volcanic mud can carry boulders, trucks, buildings, and even roads and bridges. The amount of water and ice near an erupting volcano affects the size and number of lahars.

LAVA FLOWS

Lava flows create new land, but they also change existing land along their paths. A lava flow can destroy homes and other property.

Chapter 5

INFAMOUS ERUPTIONS

Vesuvius, Italy, August 24–25, AD 79 Plinian Eruption—VEI 6

In southern Italy in the year AD 79, August 24th began just like any other day. By noon, however, the ground began shaking violently. An enormous black cloud rose high in the sky over Mount Vesuvius.

an eruption of Mount Vesuvius in 1906

12 P.M.–3 P.M.

Earthquakes are felt in Oplontis, Terzigno, and Pompeii, cities south of Vesuvius. A heavy downfall of tephra begins to descend from the sky. A cloud of ash blocks out sunlight. People in Herculaneum see the eruption cloud rise above the volcano. Residents rush for shelter.

3 P.M.–SUNSET

Frightened residents frantically flee their cities. They try to get as far away from Vesuvius as they can.

AUGUST 25, AD 79, 1:00 A.M.–7:30 A.M.

A series of pyroclastic flows reach the cities of Herculaneum and Pompeii. A lahar covers Herculaneum, burying it in 75 feet (23 m) of mud. Pompeii is covered in 10 feet (3 m) of volcanic ash. There are no survivors in Pompeii or Herculaneum.

Map label: VESUVIUS, ITALY

Vesuvius Today

Could Vesuvius erupt again today? The answer is yes. Vesuvius is still an active volcano and has erupted many times since AD 79. These eruptions haven't been as dramatic as that infamous eruption. The next one, however, could be. More than 3,000,000 people now live in Vesuvius' shadow. There are more people living near Vesuvius than in any other volcanic region in the world. If Vesuvius erupted today at the same magnitude as the AD 79 eruption, the results would be catastrophic.

WHO WAS PLINY?

Pliny the Elder was a Roman naval commander stationed in the coastal town of Misenum. He saw an unusual cloud forming above Vesuvius and decided to get a closer look. He invited his nephew, known as Pliny the Younger, to come with him. His nephew decided not to go. As he was about to leave, Pliny the Elder received a letter from the wife of a close friend. She lived at the foot of the volcano and needed help. Pliny the Elder went to help her, but never arrived. His body was found two days later.

Pliny the Younger wrote a series of letters that described the events that had occurred. Today, in honor of both Pliny the Elder and Pliny the Younger, the word "Plinian" is used to describe a type of volcanic eruption.

Pliny the Elder

Krakatau, Indonesia, August 26–27, 1883 Ultra-Plinian Eruption—VEI 6

Indonesia is a country in the South Pacific. It is made up of more than 17,000 islands. It is part of the Ring of Fire. There are more volcanoes in Indonesia than in any other country on Earth.

Krakatau is an uninhabited island group in Indonesia. Krakatau once contained three active volcanoes: Perboewatan, Danan, and Rakata. That is no longer the case. Here's why.

MAY 1883

A German warship captain reports a huge cloud of ash and steam rising above the volcano Krakatau, which is also known as Krakatoa. This is the first time the volcano erupts in more than 200 years.

JUNE–JULY 1883

Crews on numerous vessels report seeing eruptions. Villagers on Sumatra and Java watch the explosions from their coastlines. Pumice is found floating in the Sunda Strait.

AUGUST 26, 1883, 12:53 P.M.

Krakatau explodes, propelling a black cloud of volcanic debris 15 miles (24 km) into the atmosphere.

KRAKATAU, INDONESIA

AUGUST 27, 1883, 5:30 A.M.

The first of four enormous eruptions occurs. The final eruption is so violent that it can be heard a quarter of the way around the world. The island is blown apart. Two-thirds of the island collapses into the sea. The collapse creates a wall of water 130 feet (40 m) tall. Tsunami waves flood many of the islands closest to Krakatau. More than 36,000 people lose their lives.

Violent Eruption

Krakatau's eruption in 1883 was among the most violent volcanic events in human history. The explosion that destroyed the island was equal to the power of 21,000 atomic bombs!

"People often talk about Krakatoa. The eruption blast was so loud it was heard thousands of kilometers away in central Australia and is said to be the loudest noise ever heard by humans."

–PROFESSOR RAY CAS FROM MELBOURNE'S MONASH UNIVERSITY

Today, Anak Krakatau continues to erupt regularly.

A New Island

On December 29, 1927, a new island emerges where Perboewatan and Danan volcanoes used to exist. This little volcanic island is named Anak Krakatau which means "Child of Krakatau."

Mount Pelee, St. Pierre, Martinique, May 8, 1902 Pelean Eruption—VEI 4

The city of St. Pierre was located on the Caribbean island of Martinique. In the early 1900s, it was a vibrant French city. Many called it the Paris of the West Indies. Nearly 30,000 people lived in the area.

Mount Pelee towered in the distance. The inhabitants of the island knew Mount Pelee was a volcano. They weren't worried because it had not made even a small noise since August 1856. The velvety green Mount Pelee was slumbering. No one ever dreamed it would awaken again.

Mount Pelee's Terrible Awakening

JANUARY 1902

People notice a sudden increase in fumarole activity on Mount Pelee.

APRIL 1902

A great column of steam and ash billows near the volcano's summit. The volcano begins to rumble and shudder. A cloud of sulfurous gas hangs over the town of St. Pierre and ash falls from the sky. Insects and snakes are driven from their home on Mount Pelee. They find refuge in St. Pierre. About 50 people die from snake bites. The lake in the volcano's crater heats to boiling.

Mount Pelee erupts in 1902.

ISLAND OF
MARTINIQUE

MAY 5, 1902

The crater's rim collapses and the lake's boiling water
rushes out. It mixes with ash, rocks, and boulders to form
a lahar. The mudflow rushes down the side of the mountain,
burying everything in its path. When it plunges into the
ocean, it causes a tsunami. The low-lying areas of St. Pierre are
flooded. People fear for their safety and make plans to flee the
city. The government, however, reports that everything is safe.
People are convinced to stay. Many people in the surrounding
countryside flock to St. Pierre because they think it's the safest
place to be.

MAY 8, 1902, 7:50 A.M.

Mount Pelee explodes. A black cloud of scorching hot gas,
ash, and cinders rockets down the volcano's cliffs at 100 miles
(161 km) per hour. In less than one minute, the debris strikes
St. Pierre with hurricane-force winds. The city is destroyed.
The blast also destroys more than 20 ships anchored offshore.
Only 2 of the 30,000 people dwelling in the city survive.

41

Mount St. Helens, Washington State, U.S.A., May 18, 1980 Plinian Eruption—VEI 5

Mount St. Helens' snowcapped volcanic dome was a sleeping giant for at least 124 years before the spring of 1980. That's when rising magma below the volcano's summit could no longer be contained.

Day of Destruction

MAY 17, 1980

More than 10,000 small earthquakes have occurred near the volcano since March 16. The north flank of the mountain has expanded into an enormous bulge.

MAY 28, 1980
8:32 A.M.

A 5.1 magnitude earthquake causes the volcano's summit and bulge in the north flank to slide away. This is the largest landslide in recorded history.

Mount St. Helens erupts in 1983. It is still an active volcano.

42

MOUNT
ST. HELENS

CANADA

UNITED STATES

MEXICO

BRAZIL

8:33 A.M.

The landslide tears a hole in the side of the volcano. This creates an enormous crater 1 mile (1.6 km) wide and 1.7 miles (3 km) long. The magma and debris that had been trapped inside the volcano explodes from the crater at a speed of 300 miles (483 km) per hour.

8:48 A.M.

Ash and gas have risen more than 15 miles (24 km) into the atmosphere. Magma, ash, and pumice continue to erupt throughout the day.

3 P.M.–5 P.M.

The eruption reaches its peak. Cities that are hundreds of miles away from Mount St. Helens report experiencing total darkness just hours after the blast.

MORE POWERFUL THAN AN ATOMIC BOMB

According to scientists, the blast from the Mount St. Helens eruption was 400 to 500 times greater than the atomic bomb that fell on Hiroshima, Japan, in August 1945. As a result of Mount St. Helens' eruption, 57 people lost their lives. Millions of trees were destroyed—enough to build 300,000 two-bedroom homes! Nearly 200 homes, 27 bridges, and many miles of roads, highways, and railways were destroyed.

Living in the Shadow of a Volcano

People around the world lead normal lives in the shadow of volcanoes. There are, however, some things that people near volcanoes have to deal with that people who live in other areas do not.

One danger that people living near volcanoes face is earthquakes. Tricia Jones has lived most of her life on Hawaii Island, where there are three active volcanoes. Her family lives close to two of them. "There are a lot of little earthquakes due to the volcano that we live very close to," Tricia explains. "We built our house on post and pier foundation because a regular cement slab foundation may crack due to the frequent tremors. The house on post and pier can allow for movement without damage to the house."

Vog is also a problem for people living near active volcanoes. Vog is a type of fog made up of sulfur dioxide vapors that are given off by volcanoes. It can cause problems for young children and for people who have asthma and other respiratory problems. Acid rain is formed when vog mixes with rain. This causes damage to vehicles, homes, and other structures.

What do people who live near volcanoes do in the event of an eruption? "Get in your car and drive away," says Tricia Jones. "The lava [in Hawaii] moves very slowly, so if there was an eruption, and lava flow is headed your way, you have enough time to gather people and important belongings. You can't stop the lava or block it, so it's best to stay out of the way," she explains.

People who decide to live in the shadow of a volcano must understand that there are risks involved. They must stay alert and keep informed of current events related to the volcano.

FACT:

Earth is not the only place that volcanoes are found. The largest known volcano in our solar system is on Mars. It is 373 miles (600 km) wide and 13 miles (21 km) high!

GLOSSARY

ash cloud (ASH KLOWD)—cloud of hot dust particles and rocks that is formed when the volcano erupts

convection current (kuhn-VEK-shuhn KUR-uhnt)— circular motion in a liquid caused by heating and cooling

crater (KRAY-tur)—an indent in the top of a volcano from which lava flows

eruption (i-RUHP-shuhn)—the release of magma, rock, and ash from a vent in Earth's crust

fault (FAWLT)—a crack in the earth where two plates meet

lava (LAH-vuh)—magma that has reached the surface of Earth

magma (MAG-muh)—partially melted rock beneath Earth's surface

Pelean eruption (PEL-ee-uhn i-RUHP-shuhn)—a type of volcanic eruption that has explosive outbursts which cause pyroclastic flows; named for the eruption of Mount Pelee

pyroclastic flow (pi-roh-KLAS-tik FLOH)—a fast-moving flow of extremely hot gas and rocks from a volcanic eruption

seismograph (SIZE-muh-graf)—an instrument that detects ground motion and measures how strong it is

READ MORE

Fradin, Judith Bloom, and Dennis Fradin *Volcanoes.* Witness to Disaster. Washington, D.C.: National Geographic, 2007.

Harbo, Christopher L. *The Explosive World of Volcanoes with Max Axiom, Super Scientist.* Graphic Science. Mankato, Minn.: Capstone Press, 2008.

Rubin, Ken. *Volcanoes and Earthquakes.* New York: Simon & Schuster Books for Young Readers, 2007.

Stewart, Melissa. *Inside Volcanoes.* Inside. New York: Sterling Publishing Co. Inc., 2011.

Van Rose, Susanna. *Eyewitness Volcano.* DK Eyewitness Books. New York: DK Publishing, 2008.

INTERNET SITES

FactHound offers a safe, fun way to find Internet sites related to this book. All of the sites on FactHound have been researched by our staff.

Here's all you do:

Visit *www.facthound.com*

Type in this code: 9781429660228

INDEX